The Heart of a Believer

Dolores L. Sowell, NHS

The Heart of a Believer
© 2022 Dolores L. Sowell, MHS

ISBN 978-1-66786-014-5

Table of Contents

Introduction
The Heart of A Believer
"Rend Your Heart, And Not Your Garments"

The word in this passage is **"rend," not "render."** It was the custom of ancient Jewish people (and other nearby cultures) to vigorously tear one's clothing as a visible sign of deep emotion. It was a way of venting ones anger, grief, contrition or any other intense, overwhelming emotion. The rending of your clothes was an outward sign of your inward feelings.

But, many customs can become purely habits and, they're done without any serious thought. When they are not genuine expressions of our inner feelings; they can become just a show we put on for others to see.

In **Joel 2:12-13** the LORD calls upon his people to genuinely repent over their sins. He doesn't simply want to see an outward display of tearing clothes, but a genuine sorrow over their sin. This is why in (vs.)13 he says, "Rend your heart and not your garments." He is not forbidding them to tear their clothes, but what he really wants is deep, heart-felt contrition over sin.

Bible verses about the heart are mentioned throughout these pages. King David in the Bible will be a constant reminder, throughout this study regarding one's heart. The condition of the heart is extremely important when it comes to salvation, your daily walk with the Lord. It was said, the word heart is mentioned almost a 1000 times in the Bible. Feel free to conduct your own research.

This Book of Study is a pathway to restoration (repair) or discovery. You can find out why the heart is vitally important for all people. Every ethnic group around the world; no matter what: tradition, ancestry, language, history, society, culture, nation, religion, or whatever your individual social structure and background may be; it was God who gave you a heart. The heart is a composition of the spirit in three parts.. called the "tripartite" nature of man. Much like the divine Trinity, the three parts of a human make one being.

Though distinct, the three parts of all people work together to live, exist, and interact with God and creation; we are all three parts: of the soul. It includes:

1. The **conscience** (Heb. 10:22), the first part of our spirit.

2. The **soul** is the part of you that God created that is permanent and that existed before this life and will continue beyond this life. Our soul is our personality, who we are. With our soul we think, reason, consider, remember, and wonder. We experience emotions like happiness, love, sorrow, anger, relief, and compassion. And we're able to resolve, choose, and make decisions.

3. The **human spirit** is the deepest part of a person. By means of this innermost part, we can contact God in the spiritual realm. No other creature was created by God with this third part. In all the **body** as our external part is the outer organ, possessing world-consciousness, that we may contact the material world. The body contains the soul, and the soul is the vessel that contains the spirit.

Finally: The Bible says, the **heart** is **considered the seat of life or strength**. Hence, it means mind, soul, spirit, or one's entire emotional nature and understanding.

I was privileged (at a very early age) to live an eventful, colorful life. I am an ex-doo-whopper from the 60" s. We were an all-Girl Pop Group called, The Sherry's; from North Philadelphia, Pa.. We were well Nationally and Internationally known. We travelled extensively, and often appeared on, American Bandstand, with the very famous Dick Clark, performed on several tours of his, many other famous stars. We worked the Theatre Circle: The famous Apollo Theatre in New York, The Uptown in Philly, Pa., and others. I was performing at the Howard Theatre, in Washington D.C. on the day, President John F. Kennedy was assassinated. It was one of the saddest days ever.

Europe was quite an experience. I met Louis Armstrong at the famous "Tivoli" Amusement Park, in Copenhagen, Denmark; which has a variety of entertainment and events. I've stayed in Stockholm Sweden,

Finland and Norway and have worked in all of them, several times. I have also lived in Harrow Weald, Middlesex, England, for a spell. I lived with a friend, and his well-established family. This family was also in show business, and had historic ties with all the "pomp and circumstance" people fitting the social occasions, in their grandeur in England. I've been to Buckingham Palace, Number 10 Downing St (Prime Minister's residence, The famous Madame Tussauds, wax museum, you name it, On occasion, I was taken to places where, I was the only black face present, and of course, I was (the mystery person) in the spotlight. Each time, it was Who is she? It was fun! I truly believe, (even then) God was molding and shaping me.

Every experience was preparation time for me. I met so many people, some very nice, some were not. I've had racial experiences. I've seen many entertainers do drugs before they went on stage to perform, or after. I've seen women compromise themselves for drugs and alcohol, around the world. There were several things, (among many) the Lord allowed me to experience. Pain and suffering is a equal opportunity thing to experience. Nevertheless, It is a devastating, true fact. People from all walks of life will go through (at some point of time) trials and tribulations. People become spiritually agonized. There are many ways and methods to escape. Some people escape in singing about their pain, some write books, some paint, while others write poetry, or engage in sports, etc. But, the most lethal and dangerous escape is drugs and alcohol. I've seen so many people camouflage their situation, or kept in the closet, same thing! Perfect example: was myself.

In conclusion: When my career as an entertainer ended; I began to drink. It was fun. Drinking made me feel giddy and happy. I would "bar-hop," go to "speakeasies," (after hour joints) etc. I even became a "Bar Maid." Unfortunately, I had so-called friends in the mix. The ones who broke my heart, I found, were those I trusted the most. Eventually, I found most of them had deceitful and manipulative hearts. I became their personal agenda/ property and was used for their own selfishness. And, I got caught up in very distressing situations. Back in the earlier days, there were no coping skills to help people like me. Today There are Hotlines, programs, etc. Back then you were pretty much on your own. You were just told to pray. Some things, you dare not tell your parents. Since there were no helping methods for me; I decided to drink my sorrows away.

The fun had left my drinking. I had become hooked on alcohol. It was my way to escape whatever, I chose not to deal with. But for the Grace of God, I had a praying family. God answered their prayers, because I couldn't articulate my feeling or pain. Prayer was the furthest thing from my mind. But God! He has a way of feeling our grief and sorrows. He does more than hear words. He reads hearts. Shortly afterwards, I surrendered my "heart" to God. He reminded me: "For I know the thoughts that I think toward you, saith the Lord, thoughts of peace, and not of evil, to give you an expected end" He said, "When you pray and call upon me, I will hear you and answer." The Lord also instructed me to go back to school. I was to study to show myself approved unto Him. To give back to others exactly, what he has given to me. He has given to me a sincere, compassionate, heart, education, and more. He has poured himself into my heart/spirit, as he did King Solomon. It is never too late. In my senior years, I received my Masters in Mental Health & Human Services, Administration & Delivery.

I have a heart, and a genuine concern for others. Amen.

Dolores (Dee) L. Sowell, M.HS/DA

Part 1

"The Heart of a Believer"

You will get to know King David, just as God did.

"A Man After God's Own Heart"

* *

God Testified about King David, saying

"I have found David the son of Jesse,
a man after mine own heart'
which shall fulfill all my will." Acts 13:22

* *

Week 1-10 Lesson Titles are the 10 Reasons, David was favored by God. week 11-12 Lessons on The Fool & the Believer.

Each Week consists of
Scripture Reading & Fill in blanks for the scriptures given.

Testing is required!

We will also examine 10 reasons why David is Called, "A Man After God's Own Heart"

Acts 13:22 says, "After removing Saul, he made David their king.

He testified concerning him:

'I have found David son of Jesse a man after my own heart; which shall fulfil all my will.

King David ‹ *in the Scriptures* › will be our "key person" in modeling the heart.

Ten words describe the heart of David as seen in his own writings:

(All **verses** are KJV)

- **HUMBLE** "Lowborn men are but a breath, the highborn are but a lie. If weighed on a balance, they are nothing; together they are only a breath". **Psalm 62:9**

- **REVERENT** "I call to the Lord, who is worthy of praise, and I am saved from my enemies". **Psalm 18:3**

- **RESPECTFUL** "Be merciful to me, O Lord, for I am in distress; my eyes grow weak with sorrow, my soul and my body with grief." **Psalm 31:9**

- **TRUSTING** "The LORD is my light and my salvation – whom shall I fear? The LORD is the stronghold of my life – of whom shall I be afraid?" **Psalm 27:1**

- **LOVING** "I love you, Lord, my strength". **Psalm 18:1**

- **DEVOTED** "Fill my heart with joy when their grain and new wine abound". **Psalm 4:7**

- **RECOGNITION** "I will praise you, O Lord, with all my heart; I will tell of all your wonders." **Psalm 9:1**

- **FAITHFUL** "Surely goodness and love will follow me all the days of my life, and I will dwell in the house of the LORD forever." **Psalm 23:6**

- **OBEDIENT** "Give me understanding, so that I may keep your law and obey it with all my heart." **Psalm 119:34**

- **REPENTANT** "For the sake of your name, Lord, forgive my iniquity, though it is great. **Psalm 25:11**

David's example is a great road map for
how we are to live our lives.

Week 1

What Kind of Heart Does God See in You?
Lesson on Humility

I. Definition

1. Humility is stated as being "unsolved", a liberation from consciousness of self, a form of temperance that is neither having pride nor indulging in serf-deprecation.

2. Confess your sins to the Lord, give up whatever is burdening you, and be willing to leave it at the cross. Much too often, we give something up to God and try to take it right back when we get stressed about it. Once you take it to the cross, leave it there. It's not easy to humble yourself... but it is.

II. Memory Scripture

1. **Peter 5:6-7** – "Humble yourselves therefore under the almighty hand of God, that he may exalt you in do time."

III. Fill in Scriptures (on reverse side)

- **2 Chronicles 7:14**
- **2 Chronicles 34:27**
- **Isaiah 5:15**
- **Isaiah 10:13**
- **Psalm 10:12**
- **Peter 5:5**

IV. Vocabulary Words

1. **Grace**

2. **Pride**

3. **Honor**

4. **Disgrace**

5. **Confess**

6. **Submit**

V. Fill in the blank spaces for each Scripture

1. **2 Chronicles 7:14** - "If my _____ which are called by my name, shall_____ and pray, and seek my face, and turn from their _____ ways, then will I hear from heaven, and will _____ their sin, and will _____ their land".

2. **2 Chronicles 34:27** - "Because thine _____ and thou didst humble thyself before God, when thou heardest his words against this place, and against the inhabitants thereof, and _____ _____ before me, and didst _____, and weep before me; I have even heard thee also, saith the Lord".

3. **Isaiah 5:15** - "And the _____ shall be brought down, and the _____ shall be humbled, and the _____ shall be humbled".

4. **Isaiah 10:13** - "Behold, the Lord, the Lord of hosts, shall lop the bough with terror: and the _____ of stature shall be _____, and the_____ shall be humbled".

5. **Psalm 10:12** – "_____, O Lord; O God, I
_____: forget not the _____".

6. **1 Peter 5:5** – "Likewise, ye younger, _____
yourselves unto the elder. Yea, all of you be subject
one to another, and be _____y: for God
_____. "and _____ to the humbled.".

Week 2
What Kind of Heart Does God See in You?
Lesson on Reverent

I. Definition

1. Reverent is stated as being/feeling, exhibiting or characterized by reverence; deeply respectful: a reverent greeting.

2. To value or regard the worth of people and things and to treat them with consideration, care and concern, i.e. The Lord is worthy of our praise and respect.

II. Memory Scripture

1. **Hebrew 12:28** – "Wherefore we receiving a kingdom which cannot be moved, let us have grace, whereby we may serve God acceptably with reverence and godly fear.

III. Fill in Scriptures (on reverse side)

1. **Leviticus 19:3**
2. **Psalms 2:11**
3. **Psalm 4:4**
4. **Psalm 5:7**
5. **Hosea 3:5**
6. **Ephesians 5:21**

IV. Vocabulary Words:

1. Sabbath

2. Trembling

3. Awe

4. Abhorreth

5. Bow

V. Fill in the blank spaces for each Scripture

1. **Leviticus 19:3** – " _____ every man his
_____ , and his _____, and keep my
_____: I am the LORD your God."

2. **Psalm 2:11** – " Serve the LORD with fear, and rejoice with
_____.".

3. **Psalms 4:4** – "Stand in _____ and sin not
_____ with you own _____ upon your
bed, and be still."

4. **Psalm 5:7** – "But I, by your _____, can come
into your house; in_____ I _____
down toward your holy temple."

5. **Hosea 3:5** – "Afterward shall the children of
Israel return, and seek the Lord their God, and
_____; and shall _____ the
Lord and his _____ in the latter days"

6. **Ephesians 5:21** – "And further, _____ to
one another out of _____ for Christ."

Week 3

What Kind of Heart Does God See in You?
Lesson on Respectful

I. Definition

1. Respect is an assumption of good faith and competence in another person or in the whole of oneself. Depth of integrity, trust, complementary moral values, and skill are necessary components.

2. Respect for the Lord, Deuteronomy 6:4-5 "Hear, O Israel: The LORD our God, the LORD is one. You shall love the LORD your God with all your heart and with all your soul and with all your might.

II. Memory Scripture:

1. **Acts 10:34** – "Then Peter opened his mouth, and said, of a truth I perceive that God is no respecter of persons, God shows no partiality.

II. Fill in Scriptures (on reverse side)

1. **Ezekiel 36:27**
2. **Ezekiel 36:29-30**
3. **Samuel 16:7**
4. **Proverbs 23:7**
5. **Psalms 57:7**
6. **Luke 6:45**

Vocabulary

1. **Render**

2. **Promise**

3. **Abundance**

4. **Statutes**

5. **Famine**

V. Fill in the blank spaces for each Scripture

1. **Ezekiel 36:27** – "And I will put my _____ within you, and cause you to walk in my _____, and ye shall keep my _____, and do them."

2. **Ezekiel 36:29** (a promise) – "I will also save you from all your _____: and I will call for _____, and will increase it, and lay no _____ upon you."

3. **Psalm 57:7** – "My heart is _____, O God, my heart is fixed. I will _____ sing and give _____."

4. **Luke 6:45** – "Out of the _____ of the Heart the _____."

5. **Romans 13:1** – "Everyone must submit to _____. For all _____ comes from God, and those in _____ of authority have been _____."

6. **Romans 13:7** – "_____ therefore to al their dues: _____ to whom tribute is due: _____ to whom _____; fear to whom fear; _____ to whom _____."

Week 4

What Kind of Heart Does God See in You?
Lesson on Trusting

I. Definition

1. Trust is a set of behaviors, such as acting in ways that depend on another. Trust is a belief in a probability that a person will behave in certain ways. Trust is an abstract mentalattitude toward…

2. Confidence; a reliance or resting of the mind on the integrity, veracity, justice, friendship or other sound principle of another person.

II. Memory Scripture:

1. **Psalms 25:2** – "O my God, I trust in thee: let me not be ashamed, let not mine enemies triumph over me."

III. Fill in Scriptures (on reverse side)

1. **Numbers 74:11**
2. **Numbers 20:12**
3. **Samuel 22:31**
4. **Job 15:31**
5. **Psalms 34:22**

IV. Vocabulary Words

1. **Despise**

2. **Assembly**

3. **Buckler**

4. **Vanity**

5. **Triumph**

V. Fill in the blank spaces for each Scripture

1. **Numbers 14:11** - "The Lord said to Moses, "How long will these people _____? How long will they not _____ in Me despite all the signs I have performed among them?"

2. **Numbers 20:12** - "But the Lord said to Moses and Aaron, "Because you did not _____ Me to show My holiness in the sight of the Israelites, you will not Bring this _____ into the land I have given them."

3. **Samuel 22:31** - "As for God, his way is perfect; the word of the LORD is tried: he is a _____ to all them that _____ in him."

4. **Job 15:31** - "Let not him that is deceived_____ in _____: for _____ shall be his recompense."

5. **Psalm 34:22** - "The LORD _____ the soul of his _____: and none of them that _____ in him shall be desolate."

6. **Psalm 36:7** - "How excellent is thy _____, O God! therefore the children of men put their _____ under the shadow of thy wings."

Week 5
What Kind of Heart Does God See in You?
Lesson on Love

I. Definition

1. The first and most important thing we must recognize about love is that it is all about God.

2. In the most basic sense, love is the emotion felt and actions performed by someone concerned for the well-being of another person. Love involves affection, compassion, care, and self-sacrifice. Love originates in the Triune Godhead, within the eternal relationship that exists among the Father, Son, and Holy Spirit (I John 4:7-8).

II. Memory Scripture:

1. **1 John 4:7** - "Beloved, let us love one another: for love is of God; and every one that loveth is born of God, and knoweth God." III. Fill in Scriptures (on reverse side)

2. **I John 4:18 John 4:20**

3. **John 13:34**

4. **Romans 8:28**

5. **Romans 8:39**

6. **Colossians 3:14**

III. Vocabulary Words

1. **Fear**

2. **Commandment**

3. **Liar**

4. **Bond**

5. **Perfectness**

IV. Fill in the blank spaces for each Scripture

1. **1 John 4:18** - "There is no _____ in love. But _____ love drives out fear, because fear has to do with punishment. The one who _____ is not made _____ in love."

2. **1 John 4:20** - "If a man say, I _____ God, and _____ his brother, He iis a _____: for he that loveth not his brother whom he hath _____, how can he love God whom he hath _____?"

3. **John 13:34** - "A new _____ I give you: _____ one another. As I have _____ you, so you must _____ one another."

4. **Romans 8:28** - "And we know that in _____ God works for the good of those who _____, who have _____ according to his _____."

5. **Romans 8:39** - "Neither _____ nor _____, nor _____ else in all creation, will _____ to _____ from the love of God that is in _____ our LORD."

6. **Colossians 3:14** - "And above all these things
_____which is the _____

of _____."

Week 6

What Kind of Heart Does God See in You?
Lesson on Devotion

I. Definition

1. The state of being dedicated, consecrated, or solemnly set apart for a particular purpose.

2. A solemn attention to the Supreme Being in worship; a yielding of the heart and affections to God, with reverence, faith and piety, in religious duties, particularly in prayer and meditation; devoutness. A goal in Christianity: Our main goal in Christianity is to be a fully devoted Christ follower, in which our words, actions, and motives reflect those of Jesus. Baby steps to full devotion: Since the goal of full devotion takes years of hard work to reach, we must take baby steps.

II. Memory Scripture:

1. **Luke 16:13** – "No servant can serve two masters, for either he will hate the one and love the other, or he will hold to the one (be devoted) and despise the other. You cannot serve God and mammon. (money)."

III. Fill in Scriptures (on reverse side)

1. **1 Kings 8:61**

2. **Ecclesiastes 12:2**

3. **Jeremiah 2:2**

4. **1 Corinthians 7:34**

5. **1 Corinthians 7:35 2 Corinthians 11:13**

IV. Vocabulary Words:

1. **Undistracted**

2. **Craftiness**

3. **Restraint**

4. **Beguiled**

5. **Purity**

V. Fill in the blank spaces for each Scripture

1. **1 Kings 8:61** - "Let your _____ therefore be perfect with the Lord our God, to walk in his
   _____, and keep his _____, as this
   day."

2. **Ecclesiastes 12:12** " And if one _____
   against him, two shall withstand him; and a
   _____cord is not quickly broken"

3. **Jeremiah 2:2** - "Go and cry in the ears of Jerusalem,
   saying, Thus saith the LORD; I _____ thee, the
   kindness of thy youth, the love of thine espousals, when
   thou wentest after me in the _____in a land that
   was not sown.

4. **1 Corinthians 7:34** – "Let your heart therefore be
    _____ to the Lord our God, to walk in His stat-
    utes and to keep His _____, as at this day."

5. **1 Corinthians 7:35** – "This I say for your own benefit; not
    to put a _____ upon you, but to promote what
    is appropriate and to secure _____ devotion to
    the Lord."

6. **2 Corinthians 11:3** – "But I _____ lest by any means,
    as the _____ beguiled Eve through
    his _____, so your minds should be
    _____ from the simplicity that is in Christ.

Week 7

What Kind of Heart Does God See in You?
Lesson on Recognition
(aka Acknowledgement)

I. Definition

1. To recall the identity of a person or thing previously known; to recover or recall knowledge of.

2. To avow/confirm acknowledgement of; to allow that one knows; to consent to admit, hold, or the like; to admit with a formal acknowledgment; as, to recognize an obligation; to recognize a consul. Recognition to our God.

II. Memory Scripture:

1. **Psalm 32:5** – "I acknowledged my sin unto thee, and mine iniquity have I not hid. I said, I will confess my transgressions unto the LORD; and thou forgavest the iniquity of my sin."

III. Fill in Scriptures (on reverse side)

1. **Psalm 3:6**
2. **Psalm 51:3**
3. **Psalm 99:8**
4. **Isaiah 33:13**
5. **Isaiah 61:9**
6. **Jeremiah 14:20**

IV. Vocabulary Words:

1. **Iniquity**

2. **Acknowledge**

3. **Transgressions 4.Gentiles**

4. **Forgavast**

V. Fill in the blank spaces for each Scripture

1. **Psalm 3:6** – "In all thy ways _____ him, and he shall _____ thy paths."

2. **Psalm 51:3** – "For I acknowledge my _____: and by sin is ever before me."

3. **Psalm 99:8** – "Thou answeredst them, O LORD our God: thou wast a God that _____ them, though thou tookest _____ of their _____inventions.

4. **Isaiah 33:13** – "Hear, you *who are* afar off, what I have done; And you who are near, _____ My might."

5. **Isaiah 61:9** – "And their seed shall be known among the _____, and their _____ among the people: all that see them shall acknowledge them, that they are the seed which the Lord hath blessed."

6. **Jeremiah 14:20** – "We acknowledge, O LORD, our _____ *And* the _____ of our fathers, For we have sinned against You."

Week 8

What Kind of Heart Does God See in You?
Lesson on Faith/Faithfulness

King David's request: "Hear my prayer, O LORD, give ear to my supplications: in thy **faithfulness** answer me, and in thy righteousness. David knew, God was faithful and just in the time of adversities. Great is thy faithfulness of God." – Lamentation 3:23

I. Definition

1. Faithfulness is one of the characteristics of God's ethical nature. It denotes the firmness or constancy of God in His relations with men, especially with His people. It is accordingly, one aspect of God's truth and of His unchangeableness.

2. We must have unchangeable faith also, because without it, it is impossible for God to operate in our favor (or) to help us. We must believe that, he is a rewarder of those who diligently seek him.

II. Memory Scripture:

1. **Luke 16:10-12** – "He that is faithful in that which is least is faithful also in much: and he that is unjust in the least is unjust also in much."

III. Fill in Scriptures (on reverse side)

1. **2 Chronicles 19:19**
2. **1 John 1:9**
3. **Matthew 25:21**
4. **Hebrews 3:20**
5. **Revelations 2:10**

IV. Vocabulary Words:

1. Master
2. Tribulation
3. Charged
4. Persecution
5. Suffer

V. Fill in the blank spaces for each Scripture

1. **Chronicles 19:9** - "And he _____ them, saying, Thus shall ye do in the fear of the Lord, faithfully, and with a perfect heart."

2. **1 John 1:9** - If we confess our sins, he is _____ and _____ to forgive us our sins, and to cleanse us from all _____."

3. **Matthew 25:21** - "His _____ said unto him Well done, thou good and _____ thou hath been _____ over a few things, I will make you _____ over many, enter thou into the joy of the Lord,.

4. **Galatians 5:22** - "But the fruit of the Spirit is

_____, _____,

_____, _____, _____

_____ "

5. **Hebrews 3:2** - "He was faithful to the one who

_____him, just as _____ was faithful in

all God's house."

6. **Revelation 2:10** – "_____ none of those things which thou shalt _____: behold, the _____ shall cast some of you into prison that ye may be tried; and ye shall have _____ ten days: be thou faithful into death, and I will give thee the crown of life.

Week 9

What Kind of Heart Does God See in You?
Lesson on Obedience/Compliance

I. Definition

1. Submissive to the restraint or command of authority: willing to obey.

2. The general concept of obedience both in the old and New Testament relates to hearing or hearkening to a higher authority. One of the Greek terms for obedience in the Bible conveys the idea of positioning oneself under someone by submitting to their authority and command. Another Greek word for obey in the New Testament means "to trust."

II. Memory Scripture:

1. **2 Corinthians 10:5** – "Casting down imaginations, and every high thing that exalteth itself against the knowledge of God, and bringing into captivity every thought to the obedience of Christ."

III. Fill in Scripture (on reverse side)

1. Exodus 23:22

2. Jeremiah 7:23

3. Acts 5:29

4. Philippians 2:8

5. 1 Thessalonians l:8

6. Hebrews 5:8

IV. Vocabulary Words:

1. Adversary

2. Retribution

3. Imaginations

4. Sanctifications

5. Heed

V. Fill in the blank spaces for each Scripture

1. Exodus23:22 - "But if thou shalt indeed _____ his voice, and do all that I Speak then I will be an enemy unto thine enemies, and an _____ unto thine adversaries"

2. Jeremiah 7:23 - "But this thing commanded I them, saying, _____ my voice, and I will be your God, and ye shall be my people: and walk ye in all the ways that I have _____ you, that it may be well unto you."

3. **Acts 5:29** - "Then Peter and the [other] _____ answered and said, We ought to _____ God rather than man".

4. **Philippians 2:8** - "Being found in fashion as a man, He _____ Himself by becoming _____ to the point of death, even death on a cross."

5. **2 Thessalonians 1:8** - "in flaming fire taking _____ on them that know not _____, and that _____ not the gospel of our Lord Jesus Christ

6. **Hebrews 5:8** - "Though he were a son, yet learned he _____ by the things which he suffered;"

Week 10

What Kind of Heart Does God See in You?
Lesson on Repentant/Sorry

I. Definition

1. Repentance is the activity of reviewing one's actions and feeling contrition or regret for past wrongs, which is accompanied by commitment to and actual actions that show and prove a change for the better. In Islam it is often defined as an action, turning away from self-serving activities and turning to God, to walk in his ways. Our Sin is offensive to God.

2. In its fullest sense, it is a term for a complete change of orientation involving a judgment upon the past and a deliberate redirection for the future."

II. Memory Scripture:

1. **Luke 5:32** – "I have not come to call the righteous but sinners to repentance."

III. Fill in Scripture (on reverse side)

1. **Matthew 4:17**
2. **Mark 1:4**
3. **Luke 3:3**
4. **Acts 2:38**
5. **2 Peter 3:9**

6. **Revelations 2:5**

IV. Vocabulary Words:

1. **Repent**

2. **Promise**

3. **Wilderness**

4. **Baptism**

5. **Lampstand**

V. Fill in the blank spaces for each Scripture

1. **Matthew 4:17** – "From that time Jesus began to preach and say, "_____, for the kingdom of heaven is at hand."

2. **Mark 1:4** – "John did _____ in the wilderness and the _____ of _____"

3. **Luke 3:3** – "And he came into all the country about Jordan, _____ the baptism of _____ for the _____ of sin"

4. **Acts 2:38** – "Then _____ said unto them,_____,
and be baptized every one of you in the name of _____ _____ for the remission of sins, and ye shall receive the gift of the _____".

5. **2 Peter 3:9** – "The _____is not slack concerning
   his _____, as some men count slackness; but
   is _____ to us-ward, not willing that
   any should _____, but that all should come to
   _____."

6. **Revelation 2:5** – "Remember therefore from whence
   thou art fallen, and _____ and do the first
   _____; or else I will come unto thee quickly,
   and will _____ thy _____ out of his
   place, except thou _____".

Week 11

What Kind of Heart Does God See in You?
Lesson on The Heart of the Fool,
who refuses to: "Rend" their Heart

I. Definition

1. The fool, according to Solomon, (the son of King David) says, a fool is by choice and never by chance. He can stop being a fool anytime he's ready to learn and apply God's word. He makes himself a fool by the way he thinks, and is identified as a fool by the way he speaks and by his behavior. Over time, folly can be so ingrained into a person that neither kindness nor suffering can remove it from them.

2. A fool is: someone who is unwise, lacks sense, and lacks judgment. Fools don't want to learn the truth. They laugh at the truth and turn their eyes away from the truth. Fools are wise in their own eyes, failing to take in wisdom and advice, which will be their downfall. They suppress the truth by their unrighteousness

3. They have: wickedness in their hearts, they are lazy, proud, they slander others, and live in repeat foolishness. Living in sin is fun for a fool. It's not wise to desire their company because they will lead you down a dark path. Fools rush into danger without wise preparation and thinking about the consequences.

4. Teaching them: **Proverbs 18:2-3**, "Fools have no interest in understanding; they only want to air their own opinions. Doing wrong leads to disgrace, and scandalous behavior brings contempt."

II. Memory Scripture:

1. **Psalm 53:1** – "The fool hath said in his heart, There is no God. Corrupt are they, and have done abominable iniquity: there is none that doeth good".

III. Fill in Scripture (on reverse side)

1. **Proverbs 12:15**
2. **Proverbs 15:5**
3. **Proverbs 18: 6**
4. **Proverbs 19:1**
5. **Proverbs 26:11**
6. **Ecclesiastes 10:2**

IV. Vocabulary Words

1. **Contention**
2. **Despise**
3. **Folly**
4. **Iniquity**
5. **Rejects**
6. **Reproof**
7. **Perverse**
8. **Vile**

V. Fill in the blank spaces for each Scripture

1. **Proverbs 12:15** – "The way of a _____ is right in his own eyes, but a_____ listens to advice. The fool _____ the advice of others and instead _____ only to himself."

2. **Proverbs 15:5** – "A fool _____ his father's _____: but he that regardeth _____ is prudent."

3. **Proverbs 18:6** – "A fool's lips enter into _____, and his mouth calleth for strokes"

4. **Proverbs 19:1** – "Better *is* the poor that _____ in his integrity, than *he that is* _____ in his lips, and is _____."

5. **Proverbs 26:11** – "As a _____ returneth to his _____ so a fool returneth to his folly."

6. **Ecclesiastes 10:2** – "A _____ heart *is* at his right hand; but a _____heart at his 1eft."

Week 12

What Kind of Heart Does God See in You?
Lesson on The Heart of the Believer
God's Response to a "Surrendered" Heart

I. Definition

1. Rather than tearing *your* clothes, instead (rend) whose spirit turn *your heart* toward *the* One whose Spirit lives inside you, for the great and terrible day of the Lord is coming, (Joel 2:28-32). Heavenly Father, you hold *my* future in your hands. You inspired Joel to write a message reminding me to repent and surrender everything to you.

2. He/God is calling you to repentance… Real repentance is not just feeling sorry for your sin. Real repentance means changing your heart, and a complete change of heart requires more than a partial surrender.

II. Memory Scripture:

1. **Jeremiah 18:8** – "But if that nation I warned turns from its evil, then I will relent of the disaster I had planned to bring."

III. Fill in Scripture (on reverse side)

1. **Ezekiel 36:26**
2. **Psalms 31:24**
3. **Psalms 37:4**

4. **Psalms 119:10**

5. **Psalms 147:3**

6. **Proverbs 3:l-2**

7. **Matthew 22:37**

IV. Vocabulary Words

1. **Relent**

2. **Delight**

3. **Soul**

4. **Bindeth**

5. **Courage**

V. Fill in the blank spaces for each Scripture

1. **Ezekiel 36:26** – "_____ also will _____, and a new spirit will I put within you: and _____ take away the stony heart out of your flesh, and _____ you an heart of flesh."

2. **Palms 31:24** – "Be of good _____, and he shall strengthen your heart, all ye that hope in the Lord."

3. **Psalms 37:4** – "_____ thyself also in the Lord; and _____ thee the desires of thine heart"

4. **Psalms 119:10** – "With my whole heart have I sought thee: O let me not _____ from thy commandments."

5. **Psalms 147:3** – "He healeth the broken in heart, and _____ up their wounds."

6. **Proverbs 3:1-2** – "My son, _____; but let thine heart _____ my commandments: For length of days, and _____, and _____, shall they _____."

7. **Matthew 22:37** – "Jesus said unto him, Thou shalt _____ the Lord thy God with all thy _____, and with all thy _____, and with all thy _____."

Part II

"The Heart of a Believer"

You will get to know King David, just as God did.

"A Man After God's Own Heart"

* *

B. Each page will describe:

1. What Is The Heart?

    The Heart Effects Every Area Of Our Lives For thought:
    No matter what your position you may hold in Society,
    or in the corporate world; the most "Powerful" position you
    may have on earth is: kneeling before the Lord our God.

2. God's Request for Our Hearts
3. What Kind Of Heart Does God See In you?
4. Hearts that "Please God"

What is the Heart?

The physical heart is an organ that pumps blood in our physical bodies. Poets also have a lot to say about the heart. However, the heart of man as described in the Bible is primarily a spiritual organ that drives man's behavior. We know that the heart is the starting place for spiritual life because of what the Bible says about God's actions toward the human heart.

The heart (the spirit man) is the center of a person, the place from which he/she makes the choices which will affect the world within them and around them. Devotion to the Heart of Jesus reminds us that it is in His Sacred Humanity that we find the pattern for becoming fully human ourselves. In His Incarnation, saving life, death and Resurrection, we receive both the pattern – and the means – to become more like Him.

Definition for Humanity: Having a disposition to do good. By having the kind of feelings; humans often feel for each other. Examples: Charity, Compassion, Mercy, Caring and Dignity.

Let's be clear! This article is not about the heart, a vital organ, a muscle that pumps blood throughout the body. It is also not about romantic, philosophical or literary definitions. Instead, we'll focus on what the Bible has to say about the heart. The Bible mentions the heart almost 1,000 times. In essence, this is what it says: the heart is that spiritual part of us where our emotions and desires dwell.

Before we look at the human heart, we'll mention that, since God has emotions and desires, He too can be said to have a "heart." We have a heart because God does. David was a man "after God's own heart" (**Acts 13:22**). And God blesses people with leaders who know and follow His heart (**I Samuel 2:35; Jeremiah 3:15**). The human heart, in it's natural condition, is evil, treacherous and deceitful. Jeremiah 17:9 says, "The heart is deceitful above all things and beyond cure. Who can understand it?" In other words, the Fall has affected us at the deepest level; our mind, emotions and desires have been tainted by sin – and we are blind to know how pervasive the problem is. We may not understand our own hearts, but God does. He "knows the secrets of the heart" (**Psalm 44:21**; see also **I Corinthians 14:25**). Jesus "knew all men, and had no need that anyone should testify of man, for He knew what was in man" (**John 2:24-25**). Based on His knowledge of the heart, God can judge righteously: "I, the LORD, search the heart,

I test the mind, Even give man according to his ways, according to the fruits of his doings" (**Jeremiah 17:10**). Jesus pointed out the fallen condition of our hearts in **Mark 7:21-23**: "From within, *out of men's hearts*, come evil thoughts, sexual immorality, theft, murder, adultery, greed, malice, deceit, lewdness, envy, slander, arrogance and folly. All these evils come *from inside* and make a man unclean. Our biggest problem is not external but internal; all of us have a heart problem.

In order for a person to be saved, then, the heart must be changed. This only happens by the power of God in response to faith. "With the heart one believes unto righteousness" (**Romans 10:10**). In His grace, God can create a new heart within us (**Psalm 51:10; Ezekiel 36:26**). He promises to "revive heart of the contrite ones" (**Isaiah 7:15**).

God's work of creating a new heart within us involves testing our hearts (**Psalm 17:3; Deuteronomy 8:2**) and filling our hearts with new ideas, new wisdom, and new desires (**Nehemiah 7:5; 1 Kings 10:24; 2 Corinthians 8:16**).

The heart is the core of our being, and the Bible sets high importance on keeping our hearts pure: & Medical "Above all else, guard your heart, for it is the wellspring of life" (**Proverbs 4:23**).

The Heart Effects Every Area of the Human Race

Examples of Leadership:
Parenting, Preachers, Teachers, Medical, Government, Military, Societal and much more

This is often referred to as the Heart Chapter because it has much to say about the human heart. The heart in scripture signifies the seat of the affections, also of wisdom and understanding; it is the centre of a man's being. By nature the human heart is evil (Genesis 6:5; Genesis 8:21); it is deceitful and wicked (Jeremiah 17:9). The words of our key-verse are spoken by Solomon, who is speaking in the name of wisdom; and wisdom is just another name for the Lord Jesus Christ (1 Corinthians 1:30). It is the Lord Himself, therefore, who says to you and to me, "My son (or daughter), give me your heart." Notice three truths:

1. **There is a RELATIONSHIP.** The Lord says, "My son………. As their Creator He is addressing men and women everywhere. For in this sense, He is the Father of all men. (Acts 17:28). But there is a deeper and more intimate sense in which we need to become the children of God; the way is indicated in Galatians 3:26.

2. **Then there is a REQUEST.** My son, give me…" The petitioner is God who is asking me to give Him my heart, which really means myself, my whole being. The fact that God seeks us out and then asks for our hearts, or our love, proves His great love for us.

3. ***There is also a REQUIREMENT.*** Give me your heart…....
No gift is acceptable to God until we have given Him our hearts; even if we pray, or give our money, He will not accept these unless we have first given ourselves to Him (Proverbs 15:8; 28:9). God wants our hearts, He wants us. Why is this? In Ezekiel 36:26-28 we find there are four reasons:

God's Request for our Heart

1. He wants our hearts in order to Exchange them

In **Ezekiel 36:26,** the Lord says, "I will give you a new heart… I will remove from you your heart of stone!" This is the message of the gospel, and if we ask why we need a new heart, the answer is that verse 25 tells us that our heart is unclean and verse 26 tells us that it is hard, and therefore cold. In exchange, God offers us a heart that is clean, true, tender and warm. Notice he does not offer to patch up the old heart (2 Corinthians 5:17). If you have not done so, will you give Him your old heart and let Him give you His new one,

2. He wants our hearts in order to Empower them

In **Ezekiel 36:27,** the Lord says, "I will put my Spirit in you and move you to follow my decrees and be careful to keep my laws." God gives us a new piece of machinery within but He also gives us the power to drive the machinery. We cannot be moved to follow His decrees on our own, but God will enable us to do this by the indwelling Person and presence of the Holy Spirit. This is what the Christian life is all about; we cannot live it; but God says He will come and dwell within us so that we walk in ways that please Him.

Here is an old-fashioned water mill that has been used for grinding the corn into flour. The miller is very old and his sons now run the business. One day they come to him and say, "Father, we've arranged to have the old water-driven grinders taken away, and we're going to replace them with electrically-driven grinders." A month or so later, the old man takes a look around the mill house. Everything is new; in place of the antiquated machinery is new and modern machinery. Underneath him he can still hear the water rushing along in a torrent. The water has driven the mill for 300 years. Then the old father begins to look to see how the water can possibly drive this new machinery, and he is very puzzled, until his son comes in and says, "Father, it's all different now" – and then he touches a switch. There is a hum, and gradually those great grinders begin to work, driven by a new power, a mighty current of power that comes along an overhead cable. This is why God wants your heart, so that He can empower it.

3. He wants our hearts in order to Establish them

In **Ezekiel 36:28**, God says, "You will live in the land…" The primary reference in these words is to Israel's restoration. For years the Jews have been scattered over the earth but the Bible promises that in the end they will all go back to their own land to live there. All that is a parable for us. Our hearts have been wanderers over the earth and there has been nowhere to rest; but God says, "Give me your heart and I will cause it to live in the land; I will establish it." The trouble with our hearts is that they wander, they cannot rest. But David knew the blessing of a steadfast (Psalm 57:7; 112:7) – something we need in these days of crisis, calamity and fear! But there is another reason why we need to have our hearts established: it is mentioned in Hebrews 13:9. Notice that this verse follows verse 8! The reason we have a steadfast heart is because we are united with One who never changes, our Lord Jesus Christ. If you have not done so, will you give your heart to the Lord to establish it?

4. He wants our hearts in order to Enrich them

In **Ezekiel 36:28,** God says, "You will be my people, and I will be your God." This is too wonderful to be true because, if I am His and He is mine, how rich I am! Look at Ezekiel 36:29-30 and note that God promises to provide the corn, the fruit of the tree and the increase of the field – in other words, Philippians 4:19! If you have not done so, will you give Him your heart, that He may enrich it? It may be that you have very little else to give to the Lord – but you can give Him your heart. If you will do this He will exchange it, empower it, establish it an enrich it.

What is Significant about David's Life and his Character?

There are many things that can be seen in David's character that are significant:

- He was born in Bethlehem as was Christ (Luke 2:1-18; John 7:42)

- He was not born into a family that held any special place or status (1 Samuel 16)

- His faith in God and skill with music was used by God in humanly practical ways and in the writing of the psalms (1 Samuel 16:15-22)

- David had a Godly courage (1 Samuel 17:31-39)

- David had moments where fear caused him to do strange things (I Samuel 21:10-13)

- David was a faithful friend (1 Samuel 18:1-5; 2 Samuel 9)

- David had a sinful weakness for women (2 Samuel 3:2-5; 2 Samuel 5:13; 2 Samuel 11:2 – 27)

- David had troubles with his children (2 Samuel 13; 2 Samuel 16; 2 Samuel 18)

- David sometimes did things to anger God (2 Samuel 24)

- David was often convicted of his sin (2 Samuel 12:13; Psalms 25:11; Psalms 31:9; Psalms 51

- David had an enduring faith in God (2 Samuel 23:I-5; Psalms 23:6; Psalms 27:I)

- David was a man after God's own heart (Acts 13:17-23)

What can we learn from the life and character of David?

No matter what station we find ourselves in life, God provides equal access to His grace and forgiveness. God does not show favor to the rich, nor does He curse the humble or poor. David demonstrated that no matter where you are in life, when we ignore the will of the Lord, we make bad decisions, which can often have tragic consequences. However, God provides forgiveness and blessing even when we do not deserve it. By our faith in Him, we too can be people after God's own heart.

Conclusion

From the earliest days of David's life until his final words to his son, Solomon, King David had a very significant place in history. It was through David that the earthly kingship of Jesus began. There are many things that can be seen in David's character that are significant to note. David demonstrated in addition to salvation, that our life's path is directly influenced by our faithfulness to God.

Under Surveillance!

Hearts that "PLEASE" God
What Kind of "Heart" does God See in You?

1. Willing Heart – **Exodus 35:5**, "Take ye from among you an offering unto the LORD: whosoever is of a willing heart, let him bring it, an offering of the LORD; gold, and silver, and brass, (vs. 29) The children of Israel brought a willing offering unto the Lord, every man and woman whose heart made them willing to bring commanded to be made by the hand of Moses."

2. Perfect Heart – **2 Kings 8:61**, "Let your heart therefore be perfect with the Lord your God – Be sincere and serious in your purposes of new obedience. Let it be universal, without dividing; upright without dissembling; and constant, without declining."

3. Tender Heart – **2 Kings 22:19**, "Because thine heart was tender, and thou hast humbled thyself before the Lord, when thou heardest what I spake against this place, and against the inhabitants thereof that they should become

a desolation and a curse, and hast rent thy clothes, and wept before me; I also have heard thee, saith the Lord".

4. Soft Heart – **Job 23:16**, "For God maketh my heart soft, and the Almighty troubleth me."

5. Pure Heart – **Psalms 24:4**, "He that hath clean hands, and a pure heart; who hath not lifted up his soul unto vanity, nor sworn deceitfully." **Peter 1:22** "Since you have purified your souls by obedience to the truth so that you have a genuine love for your brothers, love one another deeply, from a pure heart."

6. Upright Heart – **Psalms 36:10**, "O continue thy lovingkindness unto them that know thee; and thy righteousness to the upright in heart." **Psalms 64:10**, "The righteous shall be glad in the Lord, and shall trust in him; and all the upright in heart shall glory."

7. Clean Heart – **Psalms 51:10**, "Create in me a clean heart, O God; and renew a right spirit within me." **Psalms 73:1**, "Truly God is good to Israel, even to such as are of a clean heart."

8. Fixed Heart – **Psalms 57:7,** "My heart is fixed, O God, my heart is fixed: I will sing and give praise." **Psalms 112:7**, "He shall not be afraid of evil tidings: his heart is fixed. trusting in the Lord."

9. Wise Heart – **Exodus 28:3**, "And thou shalt speak unto all that are wise hearted, whom I have filled with the spirit of wisdom, that they make Aaron's garments to consecrate him, that he may minister unto me in the priest's office." **Exodus 35:25**, "And all the women that were wise hearted did spin with their hands, and brought that which they had spun, both of blue, and of purple, and of scarlet,

and of fine linen." **Proverbs 11:29**, "He that troubleth his own house shall inherit the wind: and the fool shall be servant to the wise of heart."

10. Merry Heart – **2 Chronicles 7:10**, "And on the three and twentieth day of the seventh month he sent the people away into their tents, glad and merry in heart for the goodness that the LORD had shewed unto David, and to Solomon, and to Israel his people." **Proverbs 17:22**, "A merry heart doeth good like a medicine: but a broken spirit drieth the bones."

11. New Heart – **Ezekiel 18:31**, "Cast away from you all your transgressions, whereby ye have transgressed; and make you a new heart and a new spirit: for why will ye die, O house of Israel"? **Ezekiel 36:26**, "A new heart also will I give you, and a new spirit will I put within you: and I will take away the stony heart out of your flesh, and I will give you an heart of flesh."

12. Flesh/Sound Heart – **Ezekiel 11;19**, "And I will give them one heart, and I will put a new spirit within you; and I stony will take the heart out of their flesh, and will give them an heart of flesh."

13. Meek/Lowly Heart – **Matthews 11:29**, "Take my yoke upon you, and learn of me; for I am meek and lowly in heart: and ye shall find rest unto your souls."

14. Single – **Ephesians 6:6**, (vs. 3) "That it may be well with thee, and thou mayest live long on the earth. (vs. 4) And, ye fathers, provoke not your children to wrath: but bring them up in the nurture and admonition of the lord. (vs. 5) Servants, be obedient to them that are your masters according to the flesh, with fear and trembling, in singleness of your heart, as unto Christ; (vs. 6) not with

eyeservice, as menpleasers; but as the servants of Christ doing the will of God from the heart." **Acts 2:46**, "And they, continuing daily with one accord in the temple, and breaking bread from house to house, did eat their meat with gladness and singleness of hearts."

15. True Heart – **Hebrews 10:22**, "Let us draw near with a full assurance of faith, having our hearts sprinkled from an evil conscience, and our bodies washed with pure water." **Matthew 22:16**, "And they sent out unto him their disciples with the Herodians, saying Master, we know that thou art true, and teachest the way of God in truth, neither carest thou for any man: for thou regardest not the person of men."

16. Melted Heart – **Joshua 2:11**, "And as soon as we had heard these things, our hearts did melt, neither did there remain any more courage in any man, because of you: for the Lord your God, he is God in heaven above, and in earth beneath." **Joshua 5:1**, "And it came to pass, when all the kings of the Amorites, which were on the side of Jordan westward, and all the kings of the Canaanites, which were by the sea, heard that the Lord had dried up the waters of Jordan from before the children of Israel, until we were passed over, that their heart melted, neither was there spirit in them any more, because of the children of Israel."

17. Compassionate Heart – **1 Peter 3:8**, "Finally, be ye all of one mind, having compassion one of another, love as brethren, be pitiful, be courteous."

18. Circumcised Heart – **Romans 2:29**, "But he is a Jew, which is one inwardly; and circumcision is that of the heart, in the spirit, and not in the letter; whose praise is not of men, but of God." Philippians 3:3, "For it is we who are the circumcision, we who serve God by his spirit, who boast in Christ Jesus, and who put no confidence in the flesh-"

You Are Under Surveillance!

Hearts that "SADDENS" God
What Kind of "Heart" Does God See in You?

1. Broken Heart – **Psalms 34:18**, "The LORD is nigh unto them that are of a broken heart; and saveth such as be of a contrite spirit" **Psalms 51:17**, "The sacrifices of God are a broken spirit: a broken heart and a contrite heart, O God, thou wilt not despise."

2. Contrite Heart – **Psalms 51:17**, "The sacrifices of God are a broken spirit: a broken heart and a contrite heart, O God, thou wilt not despise. I repent, create in me a clean heart."

3. Grieved Heart – **Genesis 6:6**, "And it repented the Lord that he had made man on the earth, and it grieved him at his heart". **Psalm 73:21**, "Thus my heart was grieved, and I was pricked in my reins."

4. Discouraged Heart – **Numbers 32:7**, "And wherefore discourage ye the heart of the children of Israel from going over into the land which the Lord hath given them"? **Deuteronomy 1:28**, "Whither shall we go up? our brethren have discouraged our heart, saying, The people is

greater and taller than we; the cities are great and walled up to heaven; and moreover we have seen the sons of the Anakims there."

5. Obstinate Heart – **Isaiah 48:4-5**, "Because I knew that thou art obstinate, and thy neck is an iron sinew, and thy brow brass; I have even from the beginning declared it to thee; before it came to pass I shewed it thee: lest thou shouldest say, Mine idol hath done them, and my graven image, and my molten image, hath commanded them."

6. Proud Heart – **Proverbs 21:4**, "Haughty eyes and a proud heart – the unplowed field of the wicked-produce sin." **Deuteronomy 8:14**, "then your heart will become proud and you will forget the LORD your God who brought you out from the land of Egypt, out of the house of slavery."

7. Wicked Heart – **Jeremiah 14:4**, "Jerusalem, wash the evil from your heart and be saved. How long will you harbor wicked thoughts"?

8. Double Heart – **1 Chronicles 12:33**, "Of Zebulun, such as went forth to battle, expert in war with all instruments of war, fifty thousand who could keep rank; they were not of double heart, they were single minded."

9. Subtle Heart – **Proverbs 7:10**, "And, behold, there met him a woman with the attire of an harlot, and subtil of heart. (difficult to perceive or understand, mysterious" roward Heart – **Proverbs 11:20**, "They that are of a froward heart are abomination to the Lord: but such as are upright in their way are his delight."

10. Sorrowful Heart – **Proverbs 14:13**, "Even in laughter the heart is sorrowful; and the end of that mirth (gladness, gaiety) is heaviness."

11. Haughty Heart – **Proverbs 18:12**, "Before destruction the heart of man is haughty, and before honour is humility.'

12. Fretting Heart – **Proverbs 19:3**, "The foolishness of man perverteth his way: and his heart fretteth against the LORD".

13. Heavy Heart – **Proverbs 25:10**, "Whoever sings songs to a heavy heart is like one who takes off a garment on a cold day, and like vinegar on soda."

14. Unsearchable Heart – **Proverbs 25:3**, "As the heavens are high and the earth is deep, so the hearts of kings are unsearchable."

15. Despiteful Heart – **Romans 1:30**, "Arrogant Boasters Boastful Common Despiteful Destitute Disobedient Evil."

16. Bitter Heart – **Hebrews 12:15**, "See to it that no one falls short of the grace of God and that no bitter root grows up to cause trouble and defile many." **James 3:13-15**, "Who among you is wise and understanding"? Let him show by his good behavior his deeds in the gentleness of wisdom. But if you have bitter jealousy and selfish ambition in your heart, do not be arrogant and so lie against the truth. This wisdom is not that which comes down from above, but is earthly, natural, demonic."

17. Stony Heart – **Ezekiel 11:19**, "And I will give them one heart, and I will put a new spirit within you; and I will take the stony heart out of their flesh, and will give them an heart of flesh."

18. Uncircumcised Heart – **Ezekiel 44:7**, "In that ye have brought into my sanctuary strangers, uncircumcised in heart, and uncircumcised in flesh, to be in my sanctuary, to pollute it, even my house, when ye offer my bread,

the fat and the blood, and they have broken my covenant because of all your abominations." **Acts 7:51**, "Ye stiff-necked and uncircumcised in heart and ears, ye do always resist the Holy Ghost: as your fathers did, so do ye."

19. Overcharged Heart – **Luke 21:34**, "And take heed to yourselves, lest at any time your hearts be overcharged with surfeiting, and drunkenness, and cares of this life, and so that day come upon you unawares."

20. Troubled Heart – **John 14:1-3**, "Do not let your hearts be troubled. You believe in God; believe also in me. My Father's house has many rooms; if that were not so, would I have told you that I am going there to prepare a place for you? And if I go and prepare a place for you, I will come back and take you to be with me that you also may be where am." **John 14:27**, "Peace I leave with you; my peace I give you. I do not give to you as the world gives. Do not let your hearts be troubled and do not be afraid."

21. Foolish Dark Heart – **Romans I:21**, "For although they knew God, they neither glorified him as God nor gave thanks to him, but their thinking became futile and their foolish hearts were darkened."

22. Haughty Heart – **Proverbs 18:12**, "Before destruction the heart of man is haughty, and before honour is humility.'

23. Fretting Heart – **Proverbs 19:3**, "The foolishness of man perverteth his way: and his heart fretteth against the LORD".

24. Heavy Heart – **Proverbs 25:10**, "Whoever sings songs to a heavy heart is like one who takes off a garment on a cold day, and like vinegar on soda."

25. Unsearchable Heart – **Proverbs 25:3**, "As the heavens are high and the earth is deep, so the hearts of kings are unsearchable."

26. Despiteful Heart – **Romans 1:30**, "Arrogant Boasters Boastful Common Despiteful Destitute Disobedient Evil."

27. Bitter Heart – **Hebrews 12:15**, "See to it that no one falls short of the grace of God and that no bitter root grows up to cause trouble and defile many." **James 3:13-15**, "Who among you is wise and understanding"? Let him show by his good behavior his deeds in the gentleness of wisdom. But if you have bitter jealousy and selfish ambition in your heart, do not be arrogant and so lie against the truth. This wisdom is not that which comes down from above, but is earthly, natural, demonic."

28. Stony Heart – **Ezekiel 11:19**, "And I will give them one heart, and I will put a new spirit within you; and I will take the stony heart out of their flesh, and will give them an heart of flesh."

29. **Ezekiel 44:7**, "In that ye have brought into my sanctuary strangers, uncircumcised in heart, and uncircumcised in flesh, to be in my sanctuary, to pollute it, even my house, when ye offer my bread, the fat and the blood, and they have broken my covenant because of all your abominations." **Acts 7:51**, "Ye stiff-necked and uncircumcised in heart and ears, ye do always resist the Holy Ghost: as your fathers did, so do ye."

30. Overcharged Heart – **Luke 21:34**, "And take heed to yourselves, lest at any time your hearts be overcharged with surfeiting, and drunkenness, and cares of this life, and so that day come upon you unawares."

An "Optional" Project

ou are not obligated to write, or to share these letters. They are meant to be reminders of the "Goodness" "Forgiving" and, "Loving" Heart of our God. This Exercise also falls in line with the scripture that Paul, the Apostle says: Do a heart check before communion 1 Corinthians 11:28. We are to examine ourselves, to prove ourselves. Do you not know that, Christ resides (or dwells) in you? What kind of Heart that's in charge of your life? What kind of Body is God living in? Use these letters as tools of encouragement, to promote further growth and move on!

"New Beginnings! Simply means "Change"

A. Free Indeed!

> The word of God says: **John 8:36**, "If the Son therefore shall make you free, ye shall be free indeed."

B. The Renewing of the Minds

1. The Renewing of the "Set Free"
2. What do you "THINK" (**Proverbs 23:7**) & "SAY" (**Luke 6:15**)
3. (**James 3:8**) (**Psalms 114:3**) (**Ephesians 4:29**) (**Proverbs 15:1**)
4. What do you "SEE" (**Proverbs 18:15**) (**Luke 11:34**) (**2 Corinthians 5:7**)

5. What do you "HEAR" (**Matthew 11:15**) (**John 10:27**) (**Romans 10:17**)

C. We're on our Way! Things to Do.

1. Write A love Letter to God. (Beginning with: Repentance & Gratitude)

2. Write A love Letter to (One-self). Basically, means to Identify how each

   a. individual see themselves

   b. Who you are

   c. What you stand for (for examples)

   d. Faith/Beliefs, Morals, Culture/Education, etc.

3. A list of "Positive, Powerful" words have been provided as an aid to help in describing oneself, attributes, behaviors, gifts and skills. etc. For years, some people (Children especially) have endured, and had to live with the hurt/pain from stigmas that had been branded and (so cruelly) defined them. That's a no no . Perhaps, there may be positive words, not listed. Add them on! You will be surprised in your new discovery about you. It was there all the time!. You were made in the "Image" of God Almighty.

Write a "Love" letter to God & Yourself

Begin with repentance. **Write to God First!** Give God a thank you list for ALL, that He has already done, for futuristic plans and promises, he has planned for your life. In spite of everything that has happened, or is presently going on in your life; whether it be positive or negative, you're thankful. You should be thankful for all things. Things could be worse. But, for the Grace of God, there goes I".

You must write in Spirit and in Truth, because, He knows the intent of the heart, and the letter. *(Genesis 6:5, 8, 22, 7:1, 8:20-22, Psalm 107:33-38. Isaiah 6:5-8)*

1. **Don't type. Take your time and handwrite slowly, using elegant script or the messy scrawl of your youth, whatever you like best.** (I prefer cursive for love letters, the shape of the letters twirling reminds me of being invited to dance.

2. Give yourself a salutation (greeting) that makes you smile. Use the pet name that makes your heart feel young and gratified. For an example: (My Mother, Grandparents, Siblings, Family members, Friends, and others, have always called me "Honey", it is my most preferred term of endearment.)

3. Welcome yourself with a treasured memory. Begin with fine memories; and detail them with the imagery of the event. Recall the sights, the feelings, and the sounds associated with the memory as you bring yourself back into the warmth of it. Expound on even the smallest details. I remember my first, and take it from there.
    This is a time of "reality checking" to move forward, by laying to rest:

    a. excuses,

    b. rationalizing,

    c. blame/fault-finding,

    d. regrets,

    e. jealousy,

    f. bitterness/anger, and

    g. un-forgiveness. etc.

4. Transition into the second paragraph with comfort. Embrace yourself with words of encouragement. Remind yourself that whatever pain you're going through is only temporary, but the essence of joy you hold is eternal. Lift yourself up. Give yourself the compliment you've been yearning to see in words. (You are enough. You matter. And you will be remembered.)

5. Lead with the buildup of your intention for writing. It is time for the epic declaration – love. Tell yourself all the little details that make you. Point out the notable attributes of you: brilliant, character flaws, negative, as well as / your charming habits, and the manipulative quirks that you've enjoyed. Again, take your time and linger on this part. Don't skip anything. You need know, what you've

displayed. Also, allow yourself to know; you are still intelligent and worthy of change. Again, remind yourself, that loud mouth and overactive imagination were the roots and the wings you needed in order to be enchanting with your everyday folly.

6. Like the fading light of a firework or the twinkle lights at a summer's dance, turn your words slowly into a final dip and twirl. Remind yourself that these last paragraphs have been something you've been holding back for far too long, and something you'll remember every day from now on. Recall, even in your darkest hours, that there is no one in the stretch of one ocean to another such as you. Be the wonder you were meant to become.

7. Sweep any doubts of your admiration away with your intentional and eloquent closing. All my love precious writer keep chasing that light.

8. After all is said and done; fold the letter, place it into an envelope, to be stored in some special area. Because, it is special and private, not an announcement. Every so often read it to see, how far you have come with change and progress. Keep it as a gift, that it truly is. There is no limit to the number times to read, and revisit this treasure.

9. And now in closing, may I ask one more thing? Did you finally discover who you really are. Change is a process. You have began to love yourself. And, if you love yourself, how can the world not follow suit? Lead the revolution of your own undeniable worth. You are a child of the King. Remember! When our pain and distress is too unbearable and we can't articulate the way we feel, our heavenly Father hears our words as true and honest expressions of the heart. Truly; God does more than hear words; He examines hearts. Amen.

1. Get use to using *POSITIVE POWERFUL WORDS* when describing oneself. These are words that are not often used, you can always add more, as you remember, who you really are. You will be surprised! You were made in the "Image" of God.

Practical * Gentle * Affectionate* Extroverted *Sincere
Understanding* Flexible * Bright

Adaptive * Kind * Determined * Sensitive * Emotional * Happy
Energetic * Cheerful * Honest

Motivated * Helpful* Loving * Warm-hearted * Enthusiastic
Attentive* Exuberant * Easy-going

Friendly * Resourceful * Optimistic * Reliable * Sociable
Hard-working * Versatile* Loyal * Funny Self-confident* Energetic
Adventurous * Thoughtful

* *

2. Be honest creating your list of things (that at times) describe/or, bring out the not so nice you. Remember! It's all about accountability, change, the renewing of our minds and hearts.

- **Aloof:** someone who is generally unfriendly, distant, or cold toward others.

- **Aggressive:** someone who is always ready to fight or argue; someone who might be very forceful to get what they want

- **Armchair Critic:** someone who often gives unhelpful criticism and rarely offers their own ideas or solutions.

- **Big-headed:** someone who believes they are better or more important than other people; egotistical

- **Bossy:** someone who often tells others what to do or gives orders

- **Busy body:** someone who is too involved or interferes too much in other people's lives

- **Cynical:** someone who believes the worst about others or believes people are generally dishonest or selfish

- **Full of hot air:** someone who talks a lot without saying anything of value or meaning

- **Goody-goody** or **goody two shoes:** someone who is always good or always follows the rules BUT is a little arrogant about it, thus it has a negative connotation

- **Grumpy:** to have a bad mood or bad temper

- **Impulsive:** someone who makes decisions without thinking or considering the consequences; doing things without thought or care

- **Indecisive:** someone who cannot make a decision

- **Know it all:** someone who pretends or likes to appear as if they know everything but they are not; someone who pretends to be an expert on everything

- **Materialistic:** someone who is focused or obsessed with material wealth and possessions

- **Obnoxious:** someone who is annoying or unpleasant; offensive

- **Pain in the neck:** someone who is annoying; a situation that is annoying or inconvenient
- **Set in one's ways:** someone who refuses to change; to be inflexible **Tactless:** someone who tends to offend or upset people

References

Edmondson, R. (2014) April 10) Ten Reasons David is Called, "A Man After God's Own Heart" http://ronedmondson. com-l2o14to4t1oreasons-david-is-called-a-man-after-gods-own-heart.html. What the Heart is: Edmondson, R

God's Request/Request for: Edmondson, R King James Bible (2008) Oxford University Press, (Original work published 1709).; KJV Dictionary. http://avl611.com)kjbp>kjv-dictionary index

Goodsalt.com – photo

Under Surveillance – D.L. Sowell

Write a Letter to God & Self – D.L.

Sowell Suggested Vocabulary D.L.Sowell

"Behold, I am coming quickly, and My reward (is) with Me, to render to every man according to what he has done."
Revelations 22:12